Virginia's Rural Communities

Louis Colvin

New York

Published in 2016 by The Rosen Publishing Group, Inc.
29 East 21st Street, New York, NY 10010

Copyright © 2016 by The Rosen Publishing Group, Inc.

All rights reserved. No part of this book may be reproduced in any form without permission in writing from the publisher, except by a reviewer.

Book Design: Ellina Litmanovich

Photo Credits: Cover Buyenlarge/GettyImages.com; p. 5 Jon Bilous/Shutterstock.com, Sean Pavone/Shutterstock.com; p. 6 Patrickneil/wikimediacommons.org; p. 7 Jack Hollingsworth/Photodisc/Getty Images; p. 8 iStockPhoto.com/gnagel; p. 9 iStockPhoto.com/traveler1116; p. 11 iStockPhoto.com/cindygoff; p. 12 Toa55/Shutterstock.com; p. 13 bikeriderlondon/shutterstock.com; p. 14 iStockPhoto.com/jjgervasi; p. 15 Mark Edward Atkinson/Tracey Lee/Blend Images/Getty Images; p. 16 (left) dmvphotos/Shutterstock.com, (right) John Kuczala/Stone/Getty Images; p. 17 iStockPhoto.com/shaunl, iStockPhoto.com/YinYang; p. 18 Isle of Wight County Museum; p. 19 Rob Crandall/Shutterstock.com; p. 21 RosaBetancourt/Alamy.com; p. 22 Cindy Goff/Shutterstock.com.

ISBN: 978-1-5081-1374-4
6-pack ISBN: 978-1-5081-1381-2

Manufactured in the United States of America

Word Count: 645

Contents

Rural Communities	4
Counties and Cities	6
Governing a Community	8
Rural Virginia's Local Governments	10
Firefighters	12
Economy	14
Seafood and Agriculture	16
Uniquely Virginia!	18
Coal	19
Yorktown and Arlington	20
Chesapeake Bay	21
Wonderful Rural Virginia	22
Glossary	23
Index	24

Rural Communities

There are many kinds of places in Virginia. There are cities, small towns, and farms. People who live in towns and on farms are part of Virginia's **rural** communities.

Farms and small towns can be found all over Virginia. Some are in the Appalachian Mountains. Some are by the Atlantic Ocean. There are more in between! They are all **unique** communities.

This view of farms and the Appalachian Mountains shows the beauty of rural Virginia. The small picture features Richmond, the capital city of Virginia.

5

Counties and Cities

Every place in Virginia is either a **county** or an independent city. Virginia's rural communities, including its towns, are in its counties.

Staunton is the county seat of Augusta County. It is a lively small town of about 25,000 people.

Richmond, the capital of Virginia, is an independent city. It has a population of more than 200,000 people.

Governing a Community

In the United States, the people elect, or vote for, leaders to govern them. The country is run by the federal, or national, government. The states, including Virginia, are run by state governments. Communities in each state have governments, too. These are called local governments.

This is one of the rooms inside the Virginia State Capitol. Here, some of the leaders chosen by the people meet to work on laws for the state.

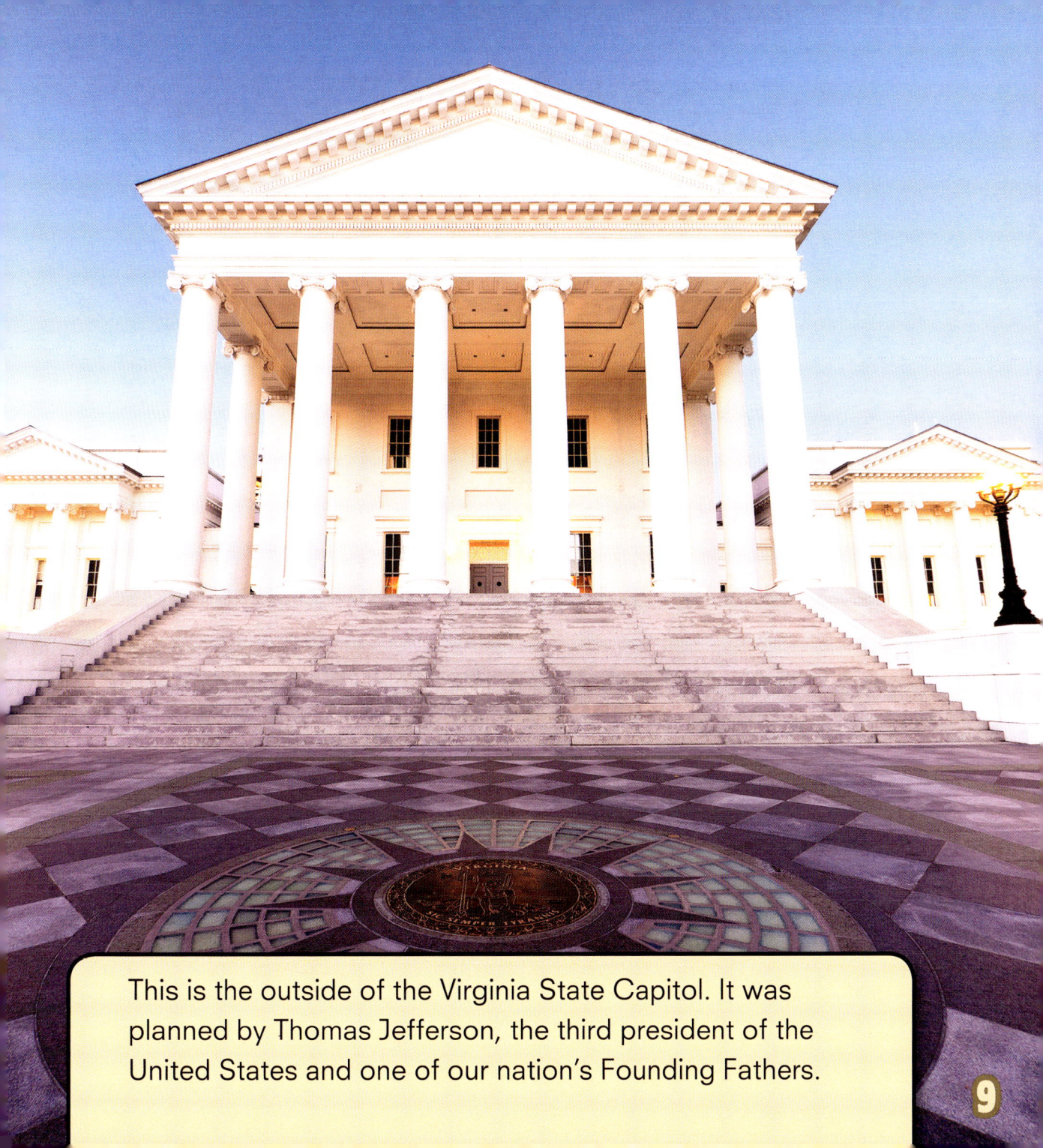

This is the outside of the Virginia State Capitol. It was planned by Thomas Jefferson, the third president of the United States and one of our nation's Founding Fathers.

Rural Virginia's Local Governments

In Virginia's rural communities, the people elect a board of supervisors to lead the local government. The board of supervisors has many important jobs. It is responsible for the **welfare** of the community.

Some of its duties are to collect taxes, pass laws, and hire the county administrator. The county administrator's job is to oversee all of the county government.

The people also elect the mayor, town councils, the **commonwealth** attorney, and the sheriff. These are all important jobs in Virginia's rural communities.

The sheriff is just one of many important government leaders that people choose in rural communities.

Firefighters

Another important duty of the government is protecting, or guarding, people from fires.

Farmville is a rural town in Virginia. It is famous for its **volunteer** firefighters. Most firefighters in rural Virginia are volunteers. They do not get paid to put out fires. They do it to help the community.

Volunteer firefighters are brave men and women who face danger to help keep their rural communities safe.

Firefighters wear special clothes and use special gear to fight fires safely. Would you like to be a firefighter to help your community?

Economy

Just like government is an important part of a community, the **economy** is an important part too. The economy is the way a community manages its money, goods, and services.

The jobs people work, the things they buy, and the goods they trade are all part of the economy.

A local farmers' market like the one shown here is also part of the economy.

At a local farmers' market, you can buy crops grown by farmers in your community. You help keep the local economy strong.

Seafood and Agriculture

In rural Virginia, many people work catching, selling, and shipping seafood. This makes seafood a major industry, or business. The crabs and fish caught in Virginia are sold all over the world. Seafood is an important part of the economy of rural Virginia.

Blue crabs and striped bass are important parts of the seafood industry in Virginia.

Seafood isn't the only food that comes from Virginia, though. Many farmers work growing crops in rural Virginia. Growing crops is called agriculture. Agriculture is the largest industry in Virginia.

Hay and corn are among the top 10 crops grown in Virginia. Hay is food for farm animals. Farmers grow corn for both animals and people!

Uniquely Virginia!

Farmers also raise livestock, which are animals that people use for food. Smithfield is a town in Isle of Wight County. It is famous for its ham. Smithfield ham was first sold in 1779!

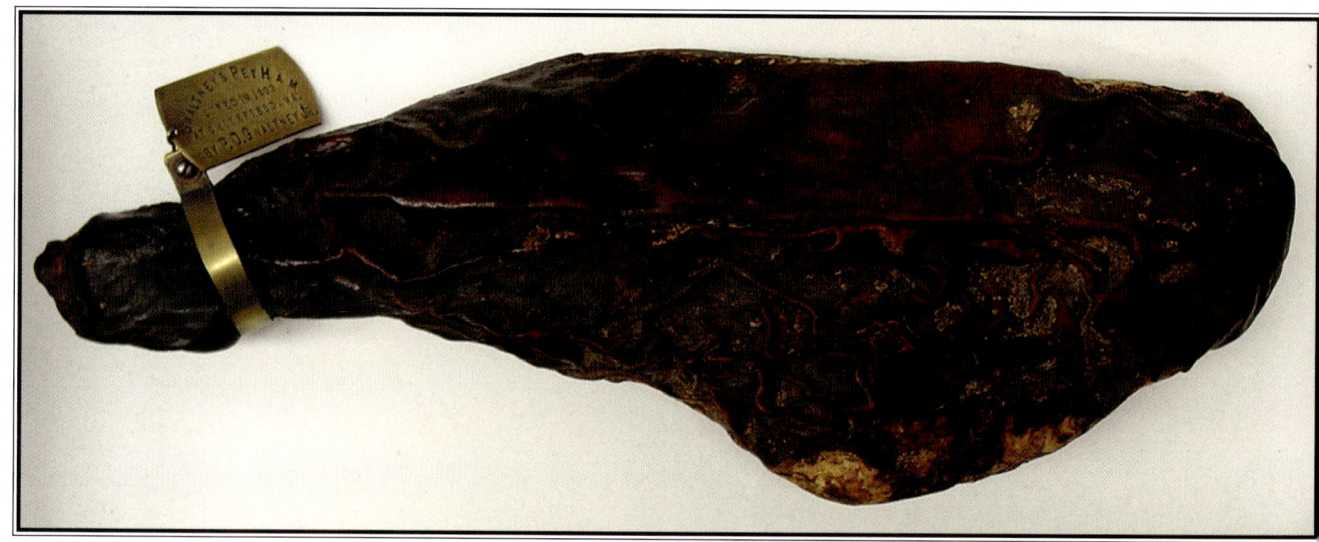

This Smithfield ham was made in 1902! You can see it in the Isle of Wight County Museum.

Coal

Another important job in Virginia is coal mining. Coal is a kind of rock. It can be burned as **fuel**. Miners have to dig deep into the ground to get it. There are very few places in the world where you can find coal, and one of them is Virginia!

About half the coal from Virginia is used in the United States. The rest is shipped to countries around the world.

Yorktown and Arlington

Yorktown is a historic town. It is one of three towns that make the Historic Triangle. Williamsburg and Jamestown are the other points of the triangle. They have been important places since colonial times.

During the American Revolution, General Washington won a battle at Yorktown. It was an important town in the Civil War, too!

Some soldiers from the Civil War are buried in Arlington National Cemetery. It is the most famous cemetery in the country. Men and women who have served our country in the armed forces are buried there. People visit from all over the nation to honor them.

Chesapeake Bay

Eastern Shore and Tiger Island are in Chesapeake Bay. The Chesapeake Bay Bridge-Tunnel connects Eastern Shore to the rest of Virginia. It is 23 miles (37 km) long! People visit to enjoy water sports. They come to see birds. There are wild ponies on Eastern Shore, too.

This picture shows one of the man-made islands that are part of the Chesapeake Bay Bridge-Tunnel. People like to fish and watch birds from the islands.

Wonderful Rural Virginia

People in rural towns all over Virginia are friendly. They enjoy coming together to share good food and fun and honor their past. Special events take place during every season. Visitors come from around Virginia and beyond to enjoy the good times.

The Delaplane Strawberry Festival is just one of many special events held in Virginia every year. People gather to enjoy food, fun, music, and company.

Glossary

commonwealth Having to do with the state government.

county The largest branch of local government within a state.

economy A system of managing money, goods, and services.

fuel Something that can be burned to produce heat or power.

rural Living in or characteristic of farming or country life.

unique One of a kind; special.

volunteer Having to do with those who do a job willingly, without pay.

welfare The state of doing well.

Index

agriculture, 17
Appalachian Mountains, 4
Arlington, National Cemetery, 20
Atlantic Ocean, 4
board of supervisors, 10
Chesapeake Bay, 21
Chesapeake Bay Bridge-Tunnel, 21
coal mining, 19
commonwealth attorney, 10
county, 6
county administrator, 10
Eastern Shore, 21
economy, 14, 15, 16
Historic Triangle, 20
livestock, 18
local governments, 8, 10
mayor, 10
seafood industry, 16, 17
sheriff, 10
Smithfield, 18
special events, 22
town councils, 10
Virginia State Capitol, 8, 9
volunteer firefighters, 12, 13
Yorktown, 20